ANNIE FREUD studied English and European Literature at the University of Warwick. Her first collection, *The Best Man That Ever Was*, received the Glen Dimplex New Writers Award. Her second collection, *The Mirabelles*, was shortlisted for the T. S. Eliot Prize, and her third, *The Remains*, was a Poetry Book Society Recommendation. She is a tutor in poetry writing and lives in Dorset.

Annie Freud

Hiddensee[1]

PICADOR POETRY

First published 2021 by Picador
an imprint of Pan Macmillan
The Smithson, 6 Briset Street, London EC1M 5NR
Associated companies throughout the world
www.panmacmillan.com

ISBN 978-1-5290-3768-5

1 3 5 7 9 8 6 4 2

A CIP catalogue record for this book is available from the British Library.

Printed and bound by CPI Group (UK) Ltd, Croydon, CR0 4YY

Visit **www.picador.com** to read more about all our books
and to buy them. You will also find features, author interviews and
news of any author events, and you can sign up for e-newsletters
so that you're always first to hear about our new releases.

For Rachael Boast

Contents

. . . It always strikes me intensely when I think how entirely my profession depends on a gift which might be withdrawn from me at any moment. I think of that very often, again and again, and generally how everything can be withdrawn from one & one doesn't even know what one has & only then becomes aware of the most essential when one suddenly loses it.

One doesn't notice it precisely because it is so essential, therefore so ordinary. Just as one doesn't notice one's breathing until one has bronchitis & sees that what one considered self-evident is not so self-evident after all. And there are many more kinds of mental bronchitis.

Often I feel that there is something in me like a lump which, were it to melt, would let me cry or I would then find the right words (or perhaps even a melody). But that something (is it my heart?) in my case feels like leather & cannot melt. Or is it that I am too much of a coward to let the temperature rise sufficiently?

from *Wittgenstein Correspondence: Public and Private Occasions*

New Poems

Cobra Mist[2]

Why did Cobra Mist never work as it should
and why were its defects so difficult to cure?
Some say it was jammed by the radio hams
filling the sky with their endless clutter;
and while *they* blamed the Russian Woodpeckers,
we put it down to the Rendlesham UFO
and others speculated in the gaps.
The sea is a great amplifier.

Grummans, Glosters, Boltons, Brewsters:
all flew here and dropped their bombs
and even the bombs had names —
Blue Peacock, Blue Streak, Blue Danube,
Yellow Sun, Brown Bunny, Red Beard, Violet Club
and were subject to stress and strain like us.

Rimbaud's Ovaries –
A Mondegreen for Our Times[3]

For Jon Sayers

Birds move abroad. Sad armies raid armoires.
Suave Eros daubs a morbid vase, admires ordure,
bids a rose adieu.

Murder sires murder, buries Aubade's muse.
A dossier – massive, abrasive, biased –
arrives. Boum.

Odium's rude brass marauds our ears.
Bravado rams demur aside. Idioms
embarrass us.

A rabid virus devours a biomass
as Ovid's rubied rivieras void bruised bodies
overboard. Ossaria brim.

Lines Composed on a Carved Pew[4]

For May Cornet

21st of August 1644 was a hot day and 'Basher'
Dowsing, Cromwell's chief iconoclast, beheld,
as I do now, the cover of the Willoughbys'
baptismal font, pinnacles, crockets, finials,
rising to the rafters like a Pope's triple crown
topped with a gilded pelican plucking
at her breast for blood to feed her young –
and with Trimley, Brightwell and Levington
smashed earlier that day, he told his men
to spare it from the axe.

Behold then this carving of a woman,
hands folded in prayer over a swollen belly,
tilted a little back for balance, kneeling
in her worldliness of linenfold,
butterfly coif and wide-spanned collar
flattering her fineness among the dogs,
grotesques and bearded woodwoses.
What was she praying for? A safe birth,
a boy that has his father's eyes
and lives? Her own sweet neck?

Sidney On the Street of Knives[5]

After 'In the Street of Knives' by W. S Graham

You, like Hephaestus, fallen and unmothered,
woke from Hope Street, Greenock to an olive grove.
He made swords and jewels for the Gods;
you took a notebook to see how words behaved.
No bare-breasted mannequins or leaping acrobats,
nor mythic beast, part-hippopotamus, part-lion —
instead three blacksmiths, Elias, Nikos and a boy
at work in a dark shop, forging scrap and iron
into the fabled knives of Crete. No street ever sounded
as italicized as yours. How you enunciate the word
— kn-i-i-i-ves — with rapture unlike any I have heard.
Steel was sparking on the carborundum wheel, setting
an edge along the tempered blade. Dionysus claimed
you for his own and on his breast your head was laid.

After *The Pillowman* by Paula Rego

For Catherine Lampert

Forty years after his death, her memories of Estoril still fresh,
the Casino with its odd collection of princes in exile,
Nazis etc., his lost hopes for the end of the dictatorship,
his deep understanding of her, his depression,
the beautiful rust-orange cloth with the stuffed black tights,
the feelings between daughter and father
overtaking those between husband and wife,
his chair on the left, the girl in the central panel,
his bloated limbs and spidery black hand
She wanted to make things better for her father
in honour of the remnants of his will.

In honour of the remnants of his will,
she wanted to make things better for her father,
his bloated limbs and spidery black hand,
his chair on the left, the girl in the central panel,
the feelings between daughter and father
overtaking those between husband and wife,
the beautiful rust-orange cloth with the stuffed black tights,
his deep understanding of her, his depression,
Nazis etc., his lost hopes for the end of the dictatorship,
the Casino with its odd collection of princes in exile,
forty years after his death, her memories of Estoril still fresh.

Sappho's Ode to Aphrodite

Great Aphrodite in a sequinned gown,
daughter of a God, weaver of spells, spare my heart,
my tender heart from grief,
      O Lady.

Remember when I left a message
on your voicemail and, hearing me calling you,
you left your father's golden palace,
      drove through the night

at the wheel of your Bugatti? Come now.
A flock of sparrows swooped low over the darkened city,
wings beating in time to the music of the spheres,
      and landed at my door.

And then you, my most adored, smiled
your inimitable smile and asked me why I suffered so
and why I'm suffering now and why I called
      and why I'm calling now

and what my mad heart most longs for, saying:
You see that one over by the bar? You know she likes you.
What are you waiting for to make your move? Has someone
      been bad-mouthing you?

If she leaves, she'll be back before you know it.
There's no need to buy her stuff. She'll do the giving
and if at first she's playing hard to get, she'll love you
      even against her better judgement.

So come to me now, release me from the ache
of missing you; and all that my heart most longs to do,
do now. Be my brave companion
      now and evermore.

Immortality for Jewish Girls

I used to think I was good at drink,
pub life and the swinging door,
waving a tenner with a meaningful look,
versatile, opinionated, gregarious,
always with a funny story
and an unexpected
request for Angostura Bitters in my Pinot Grigio.

In these latter days,
as the sky darkens at four
and the wind blows the wet leaves
airborne,
the promise of alcohol
dews my lip
and I look back on
The Rosendale,
The Bedford,
The Samuel Beckett and The Shakespeare,
The Blue Posts,

The Old Ship's double entrance and The Auld Shillelagh's tiny bar,
The Sun where we foregathered and The Blacksmith's Head
where we got married,
The Cock Tavern,
The Wheatsheaf
and The Coach and Horses

with its Richard Harris look-a-likes —
I'm still telling you the same
old story.

The Aphorism,

when first discovered is like meeting someone you've met before
but whose name you have forgotten

stimulates the part of the brain known as the amygdala

coils itself twice around your neck and lets go just before it
asphyxiates you

inflicts the sharp but short-lived pain that a piece of Lego deals
you when stepped on in the night

appears to favour depth above breadth

creates the impression of a language practised among elite societies

creaks like a ring-pull on a can of coke

would choose plimsolls if it could choose shoes

recalls the sensation felt when holding the miniature of a long-
dead person in your hand

has a low-pitched centre of gravity even at its most shallow

can be felt as addictive, yet cloys when read in a sequence

can be flicked across a dining room like a pellet of bread

endows you with a pair of artificial wings

affords more pleasure read than spoken

won't bend to any purpose but its own

can serve

when enough is enough

Running Dog

She always gave me the impression
                that she was sad,
sat at her counter as she always sat,
                her crochet hook snagging in and out
between the coloured loops with unflagging
                deliberation. The shop was all
about the fifties, (even if some of her wares
                were remakes), brown teapots,
improving books for children about
                the lives of dragonflies and medieval
costume, a porcelain squirrel dressed
                as a housemaid carrying a tray of tea.
Her enormous battleship-grey hound
                lay on the flags like a discarded
mackintosh across the entrance to
                the backroom where the loveliest
of her creations were displayed in
                folded piles. Should I say something?
Should I risk expressing my admiration
                when I know she'll barely acknowledge me,
even when I hand over my money?
                Sometimes when a friend was coming,
I'd lay one of her diminutive lacy coverlets worked
                in yellow, black and emerald rosettes
across the pillows. Something has to give I thought,
                something has to give.

Then she left. The shop had closed.
Christmas was in the offing.
I saw a promotion for handmade socks online.
They arrived, a little on the hairy side,
and I embroidered them with a running-dog
motif around the cuffs,
and as it was a thing that people do these days,
I posted them on Instagram. Spring came,
wet and wild. I saw an ad for a display
of work by local artisans
and as I approached the place across the muddy grass,
she stepped towards me calling out:
you pimped my socks. You pimped my socks.

Hiddensee 1933 – An Epyllion

i.m. of Lux, my grandmother

'*Exile is strangely compelling to think about but terrible
to experience. It is the unhealable rift between a human being
and a native place, between the true self and its true home.*'
Edward Said

I

She would have turned to face the little house
and in that moment, on that Summer's day,
would have seen the composition as a whole –

thin curtains flapping at the windows,
the shingle roof casting its crenelated shadow
on the whitewashed wall with deep-set rustic doors,

the leaves of the sweet chestnut almost black
against the sky, the tin bath, laundry bucket and washboard,
broom draped with a cloth like a turbaned socialite,

slippers propped on the step, the bicycle lying
where it fell – familiar characters in a children's story
conversing on the cobbles and rough grass.

The news was bad and getting worse.
People she had known were being murdered
where they stood and no one was saying anything.

She would have run inside to grab her camera
and clicked. All summer the boys had fished and fought.
Soon she would be packing up and leaving home for good.

II

And there she was, removed to St John's Wood,
buying carrots in a German accent – too afraid to ask
for directions on the Underground and surfacing at Harrow

instead of Baker Street from where she'd hoped to make
her way to Swan and Edgar, with its thin-chested
serving girls and air of dank refinement, to buy

the vests and pants her boys would need for school –
She thought of Wertheim's on Leipzigerplatz
where women, arm in arm, decided what to spend

their husband's money on, its palmy tearooms
where they would while away the afternoon,
exchanging indiscretions with their friends.

III

The wide imperial sweep of Regent's Park, arctic,
bare, was nothing like the garlanded footpaths
of the Tiergarten, students french-kissing

under the linden trees. And she was no longer
the smooth-skinned, idealistic woman she had been,
posing in shorts, leaning on a shrimping net,

or kneeling like a soulful mermaid on the sand
before a time would come when she'd forget her soul:
Farewell, great Herodotus and Homer,

farewell, Pindar, Apuleius and his Golden Ass,
her study, her distinction and her pride – the scholar
became the model of the perfect hausfrau,

acting surprised at other people's cleverness.
Hello, dreary House of Windsor, rations at the grocers.
Hello to the general vileness of the English class system

and its prohibitions. She collected English sayings,
and would deliver them apropos of nothing,
in an arched, declamatory tone,

even acquiring their shadow versions, so that
Is he, or isn't he? Became *Is he, or is he?* Hearing
her foreignness, I cringed as children cringe.

IV

She had a way of looking at me that only just refrained
from asking what was really going on –
like the time she asked me to describe the flat

where we had moved on the occasion of my mother's
second marriage. I explained that instead of doors,
each room was connected to the other by a ladder

and a chute, with small openings at ceiling level
and that is how we moved around and when she next
was speaking to my mother, asked her to elaborate.

Did she imagine false walls hiding families
of Jews packed in together against a hammering
at midnight on the door?

What was really going on was that I resisted
her desire to form a picture
of what this new life of mine was like.

V

On a peninsula on the easternmost edge of the Suffolk coast
she found a way of being old and more content,
a kind of fitting in with English ways,

buying pigeons from the poacher knocking
at the back door, befriending the postmistress,
taking the sixpenny ferry across the river Blyth.

The swaying grass, the long flat shore, reminded
her of Hiddensee, the old house, the floorboards gritty
with sand, sodden swimsuits flung down,

the imperious demands of sons, cobbling together
whatever was on hand to make a supper,
going blissfully to bed after such a Summer's day.

VI

Last year I dined on perch-pike at the Hotel Godewind
on Hiddensee, bought a tea-cup,
slanted in allusion to the dissipated life

of dissidents and renegade Berliners.
I watched migrating cranes stream overhead,
admired a frieze of Jugendstil design, a flash

of blue and yellow between the stunted pines,
and trudged its heathland wastes among other
slow-paced walkers, speaking in hushed tones.

The chestnut tree still stood, the house
had fallen down and been replaced.
Everyone was living in the past.

VII

You may ask what was her weapon? And looking back
I have this to say: the merciless filling of our stomachs
with kugelhupf, schnitzel, pancakes stuffed

with sweetened curds, eels floating in a green broth,
linzertorte, servelaat, liverwurst, the eldest son's triumphant
road-kill hit by his three-wheeled Messerschmidt.

VIII

Trespassers Will Be Prosecuted, was the signpost
she most loved to flout. She showed me how to stoop
under barbed wire and dart among the shuddering

beech trees, a white feather spiralling down
into my open hand to be threaded later by its quill
next to the jay's, striped pink and black and blue,

the speckled thrush's, the woodpecker's, the starling's,
the raven's, the pheasant's and the turtle dove's
into the curtain in the kitchen window.

Varieties of Gesture Authentication
for Mariners[6]

'I cannot, if I am in the field for glory, be kept out of sight.'
Horatio Nelson

To set the palette
To set the teeth on edge
To set to sale
To set to work
To set up one's staff
To settle on
To settle the land
To shake the cask
To shake hands
To shake out a reef
To shake the bells
To shake the sails
To sham Abraham
To shanghai
To shape oneself
To shave a note
To sheathe the sword
To sheer off
To sheer up
To sheet home
To sheet-pile
To shell out

To shift off
To shift the helm
To shift the scene
To ship the oars
To shoot ahead
To shoot out the lip
To shorten the rope
To shorten sail
To shout at
To shove the queer
To show forth
To show his paces
To show off
To show one's head
To show the cloven foot
To show the heels
To show the teeth
To show the white feather
To show up
To shrink on
To shuffle off
To shut in
To shut in the land
To shut off
To shut out
To shut together
To shut up
To sift out
To sing placebo

Between Appointments

'C'est quelque chose de crépusculaire' 'La Chambre Double',
C. Baudelaire

There was a black stripe in the red carpet
that prowled like a lithe and subtle animal

from the entrance to the flat around the walls
of both small rooms. The small bronze

of a squatting woman, the scent of turpentine,
the aspidistra standing limp in the window,

a wineglass on the table, two hooded lamps
on the mantle imparted a stillness and repose

in which I heard him often speak the line:
jealousy is the barometer of love.

Sometimes between appointments I find
myself on Camden Road and glancing up

at those top-floor windows, I see again
the black stripe in the red carpet prowling

like a lithe and subtle animal
round the walls of both small rooms.

Why I Am a Painter

For Patrick Brandon

I

In this phase of my life
I'm unable
to be serious
about much else

now I'm in bed I think
about the puppet
show of *Moby Dick*
I saw last October

in a corrugated hut
and when the sail
of the tattooed ship
unfurled on a hinge

we were on the rolling seas
and Queequeg's Yojo
jigged on the deck
the great white whale

hung down in the spot
the harpoon was
in every scene of Ahab's
quenchless feud

which of these
I'll keep and which
not I have yet to
decide

II

I'd be unfaithful
to everything that's dear
for the sake
of my painting

I don't even
appreciate
the scrambled eggs
on my plate

I love the infinite pains
the near-madness it takes
to paint the slope
of a roof

the feeling
of intoxication
I love being
deliberate

having accidents
I love it even
when it's
hopeless

III

Sometimes I'll say
look at that rose
nothing could be
more arresting

I must admit
it's only when the subject's
already in my mind
can I be arsed

and next is Fez
its pockmarked walls
and myriad windows like
eye-sockets

its crenellations
zinc roofs and cobalt rhomboids
the suggestion
of an inner courtyard

IV

And when I take
four paces back
to appraise
my work

I feel the apertures
of my pupils expanding
and contracting
in real time

and this is how
it comes to me
that lack of quality
is itself a measure

of quality
and that makes
all the difference
I hold up my palette knife

to steady myself
take infinitesimal quantities
of paint, mix them
slowly at first

and then faster
until the consistency
is perfect before
leaning into the picture

Snowfall in Flagstaff

*'But didn't I see a neon sign
fester on your hotel blind?'*
Joni Mitchell

I

I saw a lion's paw-print in the sand,
as we sat talking, one evening on a bluff.

Next day, snuck along a wind-swept ledge,
where minute particles of rock were trickling

in a constant stream, I reached down to touch
a small flower of the bloodiest of reds, in a cleft

beneath my feet. *Come back to level ground*
you called. You did not want to see me fall

into the canyon where the Colorado river
coiled silver, motionless, far down.

II

In downtown Tucson, two laconic giantesses
were standing at the stoop of our motel,

in cut-off shorts, adjusting their incredible mascara,
until a car drew up alongside, and one of them

pitched forward: *Want some company?* Neither
of us had much to say for we had driven down

from Flagstaff where, the previous morning,
had become aware of an odd whiteness flooding

through the blinds. A deep and sudden snow
had fallen in the night, and covered everything.

III

You went into full-on panic-mode:
our kingfisher-blue Pontiac had vanished

as every car on the lot looked like every other car
except for the number plate,

which I discovered in the rental document.
And so we set about with wooden paddles

bought from a Walmart, carving chunks of snow
off the car until we had built a four-foot wall of ice

around us. Pissed-off and foundering, I was ready
to give up, but you, meticulous, nailed to the task,

kept scraping till the lamps came on. Next day,
my face set, I drove us South, zig-zagging

down the highway till we had crossed the snowline
into the desert, and when the sun came out,

you remarked happily at the reappearance
of the great-granddaddies of all cacti.

By then we had discovered how
to take the top down.

IV

I remember those artificial painted rocks where I'd seen
many a posse gallop to and fro, and watching

from a cleft high in the yellow hills, a half-naked,
crouching man, daubed with soot and ash.

After Eclogue to the Solitary Life

by Maurice Scève (1501–1564)[7]

. . .

Having washed my face and hands,
I stretch out on the grass and study
my reflection for a while.
　　　I slake my thirst with a deep
refreshing draught from the hollow made
of my cupped hands, and as I drink
　　　I think how love makes idiots of us all,
and pray that the waters of deceit
can cool the torment of my heat.
　　　That done, I dither on the plain,
this way and that, and vagabonding,
I tell myself there's nothing here
to rouse my blood.
　　　At noon, when the day is at its hottest,
I lower my body inch by inch
into the green surface of the lake.
　　　My spirits lift, bewitched
by the variety of simple, dainty flowers of the marsh
that, in excess of joy, I gather one by one
and press them to my bosom.
　　　Next I select some shady spot,
down by the water's edge and, safe

in my improvised country seat,
am guarded from the fearful ambush
of any proud revengeful creature that may
be passing on her way.

      I crush my flowers into a pillow upon
which to rest my head and as I wait for sleep to come,
am greeted by the sound of babbling water,
like rain that falls more slowly

      when it's falling through a tree.
And all about me in this land of lakes
a pleasant breeze makes music in the reeds.

      At dusk, there I am again, peering
across the water at the wooded limits of the fields
as the sun sinks behind the trees.

      And in the fearful night, withdraw
into some umbered vale beneath a cavernous overhang,
neither damp, nor thorny – and there I lie, upturned
on a convenient pelt and watch the movements
in the sky, wondering whether the crescent moon

      augurs my advantage, or my doom.
With these and other errant thoughts
and until this moment, ravished by sleep
in such a sojourn of tranquillity, conclude

      I have no need of any remedy –
until the break of day
whose pallor shines and towards
the morning rises.

Optative valaisanne

Fais que la sagesse puisse m'instruire
sans effort de ma part
et que ce *Malade Imaginaire,*
qui a préféré ne pas guérir
qui m'a guettée toute ma vie,
muni de son pompeux galimatias,
son spécieux babil,
fasse sa valise et s'en aille sur le champ
vers des climats plus favorables.

Fais que le fruit gonfle
sur la vigne tortueuse et forte.
Douce colline dont la hanche
est amplement couverte,
d'une inattendue richesse.

Fais que les vendanges soient abondantes,
qu'il y ait une bonne récolte
pour que le *Fendant* coule
frais et clair, remplissant nos coupes.

Fais que les mots d'amour,
les gestes aussi, soient habiles à franchir,
par les plus convenables moyens,
Les Barricades Mystérieuses d'Olivier Larronde,
pour abolir les distances entre les lieux,
le regard hésitant, les anciennes blessures,

Valaisian Optative[8,9]

O that wisdom might instruct me its ways
without much effort on my part
and that the *Malade Imaginaire*[10]
who always had the wish to fall ill,
who's had me in his sights
for as long as I have recall
with pompous rigmarole
and specious blather,
packs a suitcase, and on the spot,
takes off for a more
clement land.

O that the fruit may ripen
on the doughty, tortuous vine.
Sweet incline, whose hip
is amply covered
by an unexpected richness.

O that the harvest is abundant,
that this a good year
and that the *Fendant*[11]
runs clear and fresh
from bottle into glass.

O that the words of love,
the acts too, may overcome,
by the most moderate of means,

la dure absence prévue d'avance.
Et accomplissent le voeu
de ne faire souffrir personne.

Fais que tout ce qui appartient au monde
virtuel, avec grâce s'agenouille à nos pieds
pour nous servir par ses algorithmes rusés,
et que côte à côte, la protestante austère
née d'âme Juive et moi,
nous nous retrouvions aussitôt
dans l'embrasure de cette belle
et chuchotante forêt, ou après quelque gambade
sur le rebord de la bâtisse romaine
nous nous sauvions, main dans la main,
pour la traversée de l'Avenue.

Fais que la Grande Ourse
se fasse visible lorsque je lui parle
à travers la courbe des éthers nocturnes,
ma tête sur l'oreiller, la lumière à mon chevet,
et que je donne souffle aux sentiments
qui me remplissent le crâne au point
que par miracle, Callisto est là, endormie
dans mes bras.

these *Mysterious Barricades*
so named by Olivier Larronde,[12]
the distance between places,
a fleeting look, an old scar,
the absence that was foreseen,
and will fulfil the vow
to cause no pain to anyone.

O that everything pertaining
to the virtual world may come to kneel
in attention at our feet
and dish up something useful from its store
of wily algorithms
and that side by side, austere protestant
born with a Jewish soul, and I
may shelter in the bower
of this enchanted, rustling forest,
or after some caper in the Roman ruins,
take off, hand in hand
across the Avenue.

May the Great Bear appear
in the night sky when I speak to her
across the ether's curve, my head on the pillow,
the lamp on the bedside table,
and may I give such breath
to the feelings in my skull that, as by a miracle,
Callisto is sleeping in my arms.

The Levite and the Concubine

It is hard to arrive late at night
in a town where no one knows you
and the market place dark
and unwelcoming, rubbish clattering
around your feet, and you have
travelled far for a purpose which
is not of your choosing, for an event
in which the only part you have
to play is to endure. What patience
is required of you, having been
sweet-talked into leaving —

as I was, for a holiday in the Champagne
with the in-laws, to find that two days in,
the father of my child was hitched
to a low-paid job repairing televisions,
out all day in a van with his mates,
his mother all over him when he
pitched back at the flat beaming
from his exertions, while I,
with a heavy baby in my arms
and no pushchair, confined to the narrow
bedroom of his boyhood, mechanical
toys still in their boxes stacked
to the ceiling, Camus, Vian and Brel
bearing down from their photographs
like hateful gods, nowhere to put anything
but the floor, stood staring

out of the window at the apartment
blocks or played nice, showed gratitude,
celebrated the Entente Cordiale
with my in-laws, Gainsbourg and Birkin
on the TV, her bottom thumping
the grand piano — *Je t'aime, Je t'aime,*
Moi Non Plus — while soup
was ladled into bowls.

As so often in the kitchen
of another woman, the knives
were blunt, the cooker had a mind
of its own and nothing worked.

One week became two. In the third time slowed.
Stay with us, they said, as day after day,
I unwrapped the ham, sliced the potatoes,
wiped the oilcloth, bought nappies and formula,
tried to keep myself tidy and the baby happy
as Winter approached and my eyes
swam with tears I could not shed.

Each day I carried her into town,
where my in-laws toiled in their shop
on the market place. *Restez,* they said, *Restez —*
I responded with a smile and thought
of the apartment where we had been
so happy before our marriage,
for which I'd signed the tenancy,
living — as it stated in a sub-clause —
en concubinage.

There was a certain Levite   1
sojourning on the side
of Ephraim who took to him
a Concubine out of Bethlehem—
Judah. And the concubine   2
played the whore on him
and went to her father's
house, and was there for
four whole months. And
the Levite arose and went   3
after her, to speak friendly
to her; and she brought
him to her father's house;
and when the father
of the damsel saw him   4
he rejoiced to meet him;
and he abode with him
three days; so did they eat
and lodge there.

And when the Levite rose up   5
to depart, his father-in-law
urged him: *therefore be lodged
here again, eat, eat and make
merry; tomorrow get you early
on your way.* And the same again   6
another day; but the Levite
would not tarry more and arose
with two asses and a servant

and the woman; and when they
were by Jebus, the day was almost 7
spent, and they passed on
and went their way to Gibeah
to lodge; and sat them down 8
on a street of the city but no man
took them into his house.

Out of that hostile darkness 9
stepped an old man, himself
but a visitor to the town,
and seeing them, surrounded
by their worldly goods called:
Whither goest thou? And whence 10
comest thou? and hearing
the Levite reply that he was from
Bethlehem on his way to
the house of the Lord, warned
him of the danger of staying 11
on the street and invited him
into his house for rest
and refreshment.

And the old man said; *Peace be* 12
with thee; howsoever let all thy wants
lie upon me. So he brought him
into his house, gave provender
to the asses and they washed
their feet, and did eat and drink.

Everyone knew someone in the Champagne
industry. Even quite tumbled-down houses,
like those in the bad-lands where the river
flooded and wheel-less cars rusted in the yard,
had a fridge in the lounge stocked
with unmarked bottles ready to be opened
if anyone called.

In the harvest time, when the miners came down
from the North, the fumes were so strong,
we were drunk just from driving around.
Every inch of the ground was covered
with vines right to the edge of the road.

One night, it was late, in the Forest of Verzy
my man's car hit a stag and a dinner was planned
– the in-laws would babysit.
I put on a shirtdress of clinging brown silk,
slid my legs into tights in a shade called *nuage*,
stepped into staggering peep-toe sandals,
made up my eyes, my lips and my face.
Quelle beauté! my in-laws exclaimed.

There was then a custom among people
of kissing twice on both cheeks, on meeting
and parting whenever they met and hundreds
of kisses were traded that night in the tribe
of young French marrieds –
under the yoke of Giscard d'Estaing –
sat around the burnished meat
while our host told the story of the garter of his bride,

eased down her leg between the teeth
of the winning bidder, *t'aurais vu le bordel*[13]
while *les potes* stamped and howled.[14]

And, now drunker than I'd ever been,
I wanted to let rip, to boast of *my* lost wild years,
my LSD trips, and I began: *En Angleterre* . . . and the talk
switched from cars and weddings and drinking
to Boo-king-gam Pallas, *Chapeau Melon et Bottes de Cuir*,[15]
rosbif, Yorqueshire pou-dingues, and God Save ze Quine
and a demon of hatred rose in my throat
and I stood and threw up on la *moquette.*
Next day we heard that Franco was dead.

> As they were making merry,   13
> the men of Belial, beset
> the house about and beat
> at the door, and spake
> to the old man saying: *Bring*   14
> *forth the man that came*
> *to thine house, that we may*
> *know him.* And the master
> of the house, the old man said
> unto them: *Nay, my brethren,*   15
> *nay, I pray you, do not so wickedly.*
> *Behold here is his concubine; I will*
> *bring her out now, and humble*
> *ye her and do with her what*
> *seemeth good unto you: but unto*   16
> *this man do not this vile thing.*

So the man brought out his   17
Concubine forth unto them;
and they knew her all the night
unto the morning; and when
the day began to dawn,
they let her go. Then came   18
the woman in the dawning
of the day, and fell down
at the door of the house.

And her lord rose up in   19
the morning, and opened
the doors of the house, and went
out to go his way: and behold,
the woman, his concubine was   20
fallen down at the door
of the house, and her hands
were upon the threshold. And he   21
said unto her, *Up, and let us be
going*. But none answered.
Then the man took her upon
an ass, and the man rose up,
and gat him unto his place.
And when he was come to   22
to his house, he took a knife,
and laid hold on his concubine,
and divided her, together
with her bones, into twelve
pieces, and sent her to all
the coasts of Israel. And   23
was so, that all that saw it

said: *there was no such deed*
done nor seen from the day
that the children of Israel
came out of the land of Egypt
unto this day: consider it, take   24
advice, and speak your minds.

On that grey November morning,
I picked up my baby, walked into town
to the market-place and stood
at the door of the shop watching
the slow procession of people mark
the end of a tyranny.

I knew that the sentence of those weeks,
in which my life almost narrowed to extinction,
was coming to an end, but not so
the sentence of one who inherits
the habit of human destructiveness
to the extent that I did
and who endlessly, heroically
tears themselves to pieces
without knowing
they're doing it
themselves,

and although the price of escape
could be the inability to look
anyone in the eye

I say to you and you and you
stand up, stand up, leave.

[45]

Peindre l'eau, c'est le plus difficile

Pour Hélène Cornet, ma belle-mère

Enfin j'ai pu quitter mon poste.
Tant de bébés sont nés cette semaine-là,
tant de biberons à réchauffer, tant de pleurs à soulager,
de couvertures à remettre en place, tout ce monde
à préparer avant l'arrivée de l'équipe de nuit.
Et nous n'étions que deux
jeunes stagiaires.
Je prenais l'escalier
vers notre dortoir.

Il y avait un bal à la Préfecture de la ville.
Je ne m'attendais à rien cependant
je me suis confectionné une robe assez jolie
d'un tissu rose cendré,
moulant le buste avec
une jupe tombante
en godets.

J'avais appris la couture
dans une grande maison bourgeoise à Paris
où je travaillais après la guerre comme bonne à tout faire.
Madame avait beaucoup de jolies choses. D'ailleurs,
ma mère étant modiste, j'avais le travail à l'aiguille
dans mon sang.

Painting Water is the Hardest

For Hélène Cornet, my mother-in-law

At last my shift was over.
So many babies were born that week,
so many bottles to warm up,
so much weeping to console,
bedclothes to be rearranged, everyone
to be got ready before the night staff arrived.
And only us two young trainees to do it all.
I went up
to the dormitory.

There was a dance that night in the town hall.
I wasn't looking forward to it except
that I had made myself a nice dress
in a cloth of dusky rose
fitted in the bodice and the skirt
falling in godets.

I had learned dress-making
in a grand house in Paris where
I was employed as maid-of-all-work after the war.
Madame had many lovely things.
And as my mother had been a milliner,
needlework was always in my blood.

Parfois, Monsieur me chargeait d'amener
une enveloppe épaisse ou bien un lourd cartable
à une adresse dans un quartier lointain,
à une heure convenue. Il ne fallait surtout pas
que je m'arrête en chemin,
ni que j'adresse la parole à quiconque.
C'était quoi, là-dedans, pensez-vous?
Peut-être des bijoux, des billets de banque,
des papiers importants?
J'y songe souvent.

                    Je me regardais dans la glace.
                    Je n'étais pas trop mal.

Dans la grande salle comble, les couples tournoyaient
au son de la musique. Hormis une collègue avec qui
je dansais plusieurs fois, je ne connaissais personne.
Le verre de vin que j'avais bu me montait à la tête.
La fumée des cigarettes m'agaçait les yeux
et je suis sortie pour respirer
un peu d'air frais.

Aussitôt un jeune homme
assis sur les marches
s'est levé et s'est approché
de moi pour me parler.
Qui étais-je, d'où venais-je,
depuis quand
et que faisais-je ici?
Où était exactement mon pays d'origine?
Qui étaient mes parents? Que faisaient-ils?

Sometimes, Monsieur would ask me to deliver
a thick envelope or else a heavy satchel to an address
in a far-off quarter of the city at a time
that was pre-arranged. I was not to stop
on my journey, nor speak to anyone.
What was inside, do you think?
Jewels, bank notes, important documents?
I often think of it.

        I looked at myself in the mirror.
        I looked nice enough.

In the crowded hall, couples took their turns
around the dance-floor. Apart from a colleague
with whom I danced several times, I knew no one.
The glass of wine that I had drunk had gone to my head.
The cigarette smoke stung my eyes.
I went outside
for a breath of air.

Immediately a young man
sitting on the steps
jumped up and came towards me
to talk to me.
Who was I, where had I come from
and what was I doing here?
Where was my family from originally?
Who were my parents? What did they do?
He asked me my name,
my place of work
and I told him.

Il m'a demandé mon nom,
mon lieu de travail
et je lui ai répondu.

Et vous, que faîtes-vous dans la vie?
Il me dit qu'il était peintre de maisons
la semaine et peintre de paysages le dimanche.
Alors vous êtes impressionniste?
Comme Claude Monet?
Oui, me faisait-il d'un air égaré et triste.
Il me parlait de ses promenades
le long du fleuve, du reflet des lignes de peupliers
dans l'eau. *Peindre l'eau, c'est le plus difficile.*

Il voulait savoir ce que je faisais
pendant mes jours de congé.
De la couture, lui répondais-je.
Ou bien de la lecture.
Vous lisez quoi à présent?
L'Idiot, luis dis-je.
Il était tout déconcerté par ma réponse.
Lui qui ne connaissait pas Dostoievski,
croyait que je le traitais d'idiot.
Nous avons ri là-dessus un bon moment.

Et comme ça, on s'est dit au revoir
et je suis rentrée à la maternité.

Tôt le lendemain, sa mère est venue me demander
quelles étaient mes intentions envers son fils
et peu de temps après, on s'est maries.

And you, what is your calling in life?
He told me he was a house-painter
on weekdays and a landscape-painter on Sundays.
So you're an impressionist?
Like Claude Monet?
Yes, he said sadly, lost in thought.
He spoke of his walks along the river,
the lines of poplars reflected in the water.
Painting water is the hardest.

He wanted to know what I did on my days off.
Sewing or reading.
What are you reading at the moment?
The Idiot, I replied.
He seemed quite taken aback at this.
Not having heard of Dostoyevsky,
he thought I was calling him an idiot.
That amused us for a while.

And so, we said our farewells
and I walked home to the maternity hospital.

Early next day, his mother came to ask me
what my intentions were towards her son.
and soon after we were married.

L'Oncle Marcel

Voyant que mes bambins avaient besoin de jouets
souvent en cachette il me filait des billets de dix
ou vingt francs, dans la poche de mon tablier
sans se soucier que tout le monde le sache.

L'après-midi, par beau temps, il aimait
se poser sur une chaise derrière la grille,
pour voir le va-et-vient des ménagères,
les sorties du dimanche en famille.

Il était du genre un peu dandy
avec ses chemises d'un blanc éblouissant.
A l'aise, il alongeait ses longues jambes,
la tête au ciel, le regard souriant.

Un homme si doux, un blessé de la guerre,
sans femme ni enfant pour hériter de ses biens,
parfois on le traitait d'incompétent.
C'était le meilleur de ces honnêtes gens.

Uncle Marcel

Seeing that my toddlers needed toys,
he'd often slip a ten or twenty Franc note
into the pocket of my apron;
everyone saw what he was doing.

In the afternoon when it was fine
he liked to set a chair behind the gate
and watch the housewives passing by,
the families in their Sunday best.

He was something of a dandy;
his shirts were always snowy white.
He stretched out his long legs, at ease,
his face to the sky, a smile on his lips.

A very sweet man, wounded from the war,
with neither wife nor child to inherit his goods.
Sometimes he was treated with contempt.
He was the best of all these decent folk.

Roquentin

Il n'avait personne à qui parler, exilé dans ce bled
où l'arrêt du dernier train secouait son sommeil
ainsi que sa veille, allongé sur son lit
dans la nuit silencieuse, parfois percée d'un cri.

J'aurais voulu le connaître, cet homme si bourru;
je nous vois côte à côte par hasard au cinéma,
partant ensemble avant la fin pour aller traîner
devant les vitrines lumineuses des grands magasins.

Dans la rue aurait-on fait l'esquisse de nos enfances,
au café, le constat de nos auteurs favoris?
Après quelque singerie, nous serions-nous permis
de nous tenir par la main, comme le font les vrais amants?

Pendant qu'il s'entraînait à ses vaines recherches,
je me serais attelée à un petit job, pas trop sérieux,
dans une entreprise du coin, où je me serais rendue
le matin, avec un sandwich préparé la veille au soir.

Me serais-je lassée de ses longues bouderies,
de son acte d'amour abrupt et fontionnel?
Se serait-il lassé de mes souffrances inédites,
de mon besoin qu'il me trouve toujours aussi belle?

N'importe! C'est à vous que je chante ce douteux récit,
par complicité, par foucade,* pour me détendre l'esprit,
car n'est-ce pas une mission de la littérature
d'éclaircir nos remords, nos hantises de la vie?

Roquentin

He had no one to talk to, exiled in this dump
where his hours of slumber and wakefulness
were jarred by the clank of late night train,
in the long silence. Sometimes he heard a cry.

I'd like to have known him, this weird guy.
I picture us next to each other in the cinema
leaving together before the end, hanging about
in front of the lit-up windows of the stores.

Back on the street we'd have swapped summaries
of childhood, a tally of our favourite authors;
would there have been some monkey-business,
would we have held hands as true lovers do?

While he beavered over his pointless research
I'd have shackled myself to a little job, nothing fancy,
at a local firm where I'd go each day with a sandwich
for my lunch, prepared the night before.

Would I have got bored with his long fits of gloom,
his act of love, utilitarian and abrupt?
Would he have got bored with my capacity for pain,
my wish that he should find me always beautiful?

Who cares. It's you, reader, to whom I sing
this dubious tale for the hell of it, and to ease
my spirit. For is it not the duty of all literature
to lighten our remorse, our nagging fear?

Henry James Sends a Leporello[16]

Devonshire meets you in all its purity. On huge embankments of moss and turf, smothered in wild flowers and embroidered with the finest lace work of trailing ground ivy, rise solid walls of flowering thorn and glistening holly and golden broom, and more strong, homely shrubs than I can name, and toss their blooming tangle to a sky which seems to look down between them, in places, from but a dozen inches of blue.

Nothing in all architecture expresses better to my imagination, the sadness of survival, the resignation of dogged material continuance, than a broad expanse of Norman stonework, roughly adorned with its low relief of short columns and round arches and almost barbarous hatchet work, and lifted high into that mild English light which accords so well with its dull grey surface.

The little effigies of saints and kings, niched in tiers along this hoary wall, are prodigiously black and quaint and primitive in expression; and as you look into them you fancy that they are broodingly conscious of their names, histories and misfortunes; that sensitive victims of time, they feel the loss of their noses, their toes and their crowns; and that when the long June twilight turns at last to deeper grey and the quiet of the close to deeper stillness, they begin to peer sideways out of their narrow recesses and converse in some strange form of early English, as rigid, yet as candid, as their features and postures, moaning, like a company of ancient paupers, over their aches and losses, the sadness of being so terribly old.

The path, winding in a hundred ramifications over the cliff, is fastidiously solid and neat and furnished at intervals of a dozen yards with excellent benches, inscribed by knife and pencil with the names of such visitors who do not happen to have been the elderly maiden aunts who now chiefly occupy them. All this is prosaic, and you have to subtract it in a lump from the total impression before the sense of the beguilement of nature becomes distinct.

The late afternoon light had a way, at this season, of lingering on until within a couple of hours of midnight; and I remember among the charmed moments of English travel none of a more vividly poetical tinge than a couple of evenings spent on the summit of this all but legendary pile in company with the slow-coming darkness and short, sharp cry of the sea-mews. There are places whose very aspect is a story or a song.

The Sun Looks Forward to Winter –
A Carol

Another hazy afternoon in Bath,
jugglers in the square
in yellow tights and yellow leaves
pasted everywhere.
A massive raspberry balloon,
I hang over the town and fall
into a hissing sea of flame
and then I stop and call your name:
Come faithful Winter, come cold.

Cover my face and let me sleep
on a low forgotten shelf.
Take your turn around the town.
Chill the air and crack the pipe.
Lift each collar round each face.
Let the music ring out clear.
Let fires blaze in every grate.
Cut the holly. Fill your plate.
Come faithful Winter, come cold.

Just when you think me gone for good,
the ground as hard as any stone,
the car won't start, the bird won't sing
the old complaining of their joints,
the filthy spray of melting snow,
one day that ends before it starts
such a shaft of light I'll throw
and until that glorious hour,
Come faithful Winter, come cold.

Tutti Direzioni

Aspetta un momento, Giovanni. Mi fanno male i piedi.
Cerchiamo un tavolo sulla terazza, con vista del mare.
Non posso credere che questo posto sia ancora aperto.
A che ora parte il vaporetto, signorina?

Ti ricordi quando eravamo giovani e io portavo
una minigonna stampata con i giorni della settimana?
Come ti volevo . . . Mamma! Eri così imbarrazzante!
No, tesoro mio, mi ricordo di niente, niente.

Quanto eravamo felici in quei giorni! Guarda!
pensò che siamo tornati dove è cominciato.
Fermati qui, c'è un parcheggio. Non è lontano.
Piove! Torniamo a casa, presto.

Every Which Way

Wait a moment, Giovanni. My feet are agony.
We'd like a table on the terrace, overlooking the sea.
I can't believe this place is still going after all these years.
What time does the steamboat leave, Miss?

Do you remember when we were young I wore
a miniskirt printed with the days of the week?
How I fancied you . . . Mummy! You're so embarrassing!
No, my sweet, I remember nothing, nothing.

How happy we were in those days! Look!
I think we're back where we started.
Stop here! There's a parking space. It's not far.
Here comes the rain. Let's go home.

Le toyboy de tohu-bohu
(un calembour pour BoJo)[17]

Or la terre était vide et vague, les ténèbres couvraient l'abîme.
Un vent de Dieu tournoyait sur les eaux.

De plus en plus irrité par la rébellion continuelle
de Prométhée, Zeus le fît enchaîner, nu,
à un rocher dans les montagnes du Caucase

et chaque jour, un aigle lui dévorait le foie.
Cet animal vorace faisait partie de la dangereuse
progéniture d'Echidna et de Typhon.

En plus il n'y avait pas de terme à sa souffrance,
car toutes les nuits son foie
se reconstituait.

Et Zeus pour excuser sa cruauté, fit circuler
une histoire, qu'il avait inventée de toute pièce:
Prométhée venait de l'Olympe

pour avoir une aventure amoureuse secrète
avec Athéna, scholiaste d'Apollonios
de Rhodes.

Malgré son supplice, Prométhée persista
dans son attitude de révolte. Faisant fi
des plaintes et des prières humiliantes,

The Toyboy of Tohu-Bohu
(a Mondegreen for BoJo)

And the earth was without form, and void;
and darkness was on the face of the deep.

More and more irritated by Prometheus's rebellion,
Zeus had him chained naked to a rock
in the Caucasian mountains

and every day an eagle came and pecked out
his liver. This voracious bird was part of the bellicose
tribe of Echidna and Typhon.

What was worse there was no end to his suffering
because every night his liver
grew back.

And Zeus, to excuse his cruelty, broadcast
an entirely fictitious story:
that Prometheus had come down from Olympus

to have a secret love affair
with Athena, famous for her treatise
on Apollonius of Rhodes.

In spite of his punishment, Prometheus persisted
in his contrary attitude. Contemptuous
of all objection and insulting petition,

il ne cessa de défier le maître de l'Olympe
et d'exhaler sa haine en apostrophes
violentes.

Car, ne détenait-il pas un secret
redoutable, intéressant l'avenir
même de Zeus?

his defiance of the master of Olympus
was as unceasing as the violence
of his language.

For did he not also hold the key
to some weighty secret, of interest even
to the destiny of Zeus?

Raging Homesickness –
Dutchess County N.Y.

Send honeycomb now

a page of yellow facts

3 of you parched

my pills –

(then she put down

the chalk and walked away

from the School Inspector)

why is there no real

countryside here?

Mutton chops

at 11 a.m.?

A frozen lake in the hollow

of a wood

in the Catskills

and two skaters clinging

together – last night

on the phone

such childish despair

at separation – he's not

gone off to the crusades

has he – it's so

difficult to strike

the right note

Dark and thunderous

today walked

home – he

kicking the leaves

calling the tune

of Lady Be Good

in solfège

do re-re fa-fa so-la-ti-do-re

as was his way

Day-old ratatouille

heated up

tried out my new accent

at the stationers'

the upward inflection

rather than the

dying fall

Damgate Street, Wymondham

for George Szirtes and Clarissa Upchurch
in whose house I once dined from this menu when it was
Adlard's Restaurant and where 30 years later, they welcomed me,
gave me lunch and showed me their treasures

A Tart of Softly Boiled Quail Eggs on a Mushroom Purée
with Basil Hollandaise

Crab Bisque

Quenelles of Smoked Salmon with
a White Wine Butter Sauce

———————

Supreme of Turbot with Saffron Sauce

A Breast of Norfolk Duck with a Lime Sauce

Roast Rack of English Lamb Glazed with
Meaux Mustard. Served with a Sauce made
from its own Juices, flavoured with Tarragon

———————

Green Salad or Cheese

Fresh Peaches with a Strawberry Purée and
Red Wine Sauce

A Tulip of Honey and Walnut Parfait with
a Praline Sauce

Coeur à la Crême with Raspberries

Coffee

Cancer Poems

La brièveté de la vie

Nous voici devant l'épreuve.
Ces jours-ci on se lève tôt, pour paraître avide,
d'échapper au cauchemar.

On se croise à la bouilloire, puis on se remet
à la tâche quotidienne,
quelle qu'elle soit.

Les chats se placent selon leur gré,
nous montrent leurs dos à rayures, puis s'en vont
à la chasse aux souris.

Un morceau de beurre fond dans la poêle – szszsz -
et lentement les jaunes se couvrent
d'un deuil blanc.

Dans les jours qui suivent, sois là, sois là,
mets ton chandail contre le froid.
Pas à pas on y arrivera.

On the Shortness of Life

We're being put to the test.
These days it's an early start, to show willing,
to escape our nightmares.

We meet at the kettle, then it's back
to the daily grind,
whatever.

The cats settle themselves accordingly,
show us their striped backs, then leave
to hunt mice.

Butter melts in the pan – szszsz –
and slowly the yolks cover themselves
in their white veils.

In the days to come, be there, be there,
put your sweater on against the cold.
We'll get there step by step.

Ces jours-ci je tombe

Ces jours-ci je tombe amoureuse du tout venant;
voyez cette petite poupée ancienne en plastique
cueillie par hasard dans une étrange boutique
et que je me suis offerte pour la fête des Rois.

La voici debout dans son costume écossais,
sa veste en velours noir un peu poussiéreuse,
une dentelle fripée lui serrant la gorge,
son pauvre plaid, fixé par une épingle à nourrice,

indiquant le blason d'un humble clan,
son regard fixe sous ses paupières mobiles,
planté roide prêt à franchir l'obstacle qui surgit,

sa chevelure fade et douce; *est-ce bien réelle?*
Caitlin, sauveuse, diseuse, fétiche,
fée, esprit, mon immortelle.

These Days I Fall

These days I fall for any old thing;
see this quaint little plastic doll
found by chance in a pop-up shop,
a gift for the Twelfth Night's feast.

She stands there in her Scots costume,
her black velvet jacket, on the dusty side,
a scrap of torn lace around her throat,
her poor plaid, held with a safety pin,

the insignia of a humble clan,
her fixed stare, (though her eyelids close),
ready for the ambush that lies ahead,

her coiffure, dull and soft: *is that hair real?*
Caitlin, saviour, soothsayer, fetish,
faery, spirit, my *immortelle.*

The Lions of Chemo

For Dave Cliff and Katherine Lockton

Perhaps the lions were distracted
by the sound of laughing women,
gathered in their summer dresses,
handing plates of chicken salad
to each other, the chink of cutlery
and glass, the constant babble
of the fountain in the garden,
coming through the open doors.

Although restless, they made no
sudden moves, showed no trace
of appetite or curiosity, apart from
a hypnotic pause in their circuits
of the room, a cautious inspection
of the valance round a chair. At one
moment the field of my entire vision
was filled with a lion's yellow skin.

In the weeks that followed, marked
by the rhythm of epotoside, ondazetron,
dexamathasone, filgrastin, a lion
still appeared to me from time
to time, posing *couchant* in the snow
or dozed outside the bathroom door,
registering my presence with no more
than a sigh or the twitch of an ear.

Each day on waking I could not erase
their savage flicker from my mind,
or control the quaking of my heart –
but I had work to do, suppers to prepare,
standards to keep, when I realised
one February afternoon stopping
halfway down the stairs, that they
were there for my protection

and decided henceforth I'd adopt
the crimson garb of Saint Jerome,[18]
emulate his perfect stillness, at ease
perhaps for the first time in my life,
all the implements of study
within reach, thinking of life's gripes,
its lusts and torments, knowing
there's a lion waiting in the clerestory.

Shortest Chronicle – Sigmund Freud – 1939

	January
2/1	Lumbago
—31/2	Bone ache

	February
Th 2/2	Moses printed
Su 5/2	Princess
Fr 10/2	+ Pius XI — Trotter
Su 19/2	Oli 48 yrs.
Su 26/2	Princess with Lacassagne
Tu 28/2	Trial excision & X-ray

	March
Fr 3/3	News from Paris — Pius XII
Mo 6/3	Dr Finzi
We 8/3	25th anniversary of British Society
Th 9/3	First X-ray — Finzi
Sa 11/3	Anniversary of the Nazi invasion
Mo 13/3	Moses with Lange — Princess & Lacassagne
We 15/3	Radium — Prague occupied

	April
Th 4/4	Ernst 47 yrs.
Su 16/4	Summer time

We 19/4   Alexander 73 yrs.
Th 20/4   Schur to New York

May

Sa 6/5   83rd birthday
Fr 12/5   Topsy published
Fr 19/5   Moses in English
Sa 20/5   Anna to Amsterdam

June

Tue 6/6   One year in England

July

Su 2/7   Princess birthday at our house.
Mo 10/7   + Havelock Ellis
We 12/7   Schur back
Sa 15/7   + Bleuler
Mo 24/7   Evchen — Wells in citizenship
We 26/7   Marthe 78 yrs.

August

Tue 1/8   Disbanded the practice. Visitors. Ruth Prince
           George & Marie, Segredakis. Sachs.
We 23   Ruth taken leave
Th 24   Money from bank
Fr 25   Eva to Nice. Dorothy N. York
           War panic

Poems by Jacques Tornay,
translated into English by Annie Freud

Ce qui nous dépossède le moins

Sommes-nous le jour d'une ample musique
ou d'un espoir tombé de l'échelle?
Peu importe, les heures vont se faire
que nous ne maîtriserons pas, de nouveau la nuit s'installera
sans être invitée, la lune dormira encore à la belle étoile, etc.
Il y aura de l'obscurité telle qu'on en trouve dans les buffets.

A midi, sur la vitre poussiéreuse d'un café un homme tracera
du doigt un prénom féminin et tôt ou tard nous en serons tous là,
à nous interroger aussi sur le cycle lancinant des rivières ou autre.
Pourquoi tant de pas nous précèdent et néanmoins l'on s'égare
à la recherche d'un infini dont l'oeil s'ouvrirait, délié,
vers cette flamme qui nous a toujours manqué. De même l'air
fait défaut entre les balcons qui se répondent par-dessus les rues
tandis qu'en bas une ombre appuyée à la verticale contre le mur
s'en détache, lasse d'être debout.

Ailleurs, quelqu'un tourne un bouton de radio en tous sens
comme s'il voulait qu'il fleurisse.
En attendant nous devons produire de quoi persister,
faire alliance durable avec ce qui nous dépossède le moins.

Whatever Defeats Us Least

Will today be a day that we're part of a symphony
or a day when hope falls from a ladder?
What does it matter? We cannot keep pace with the hours;
once more night settles down without being asked.
The moon will go on falling asleep under the stars etc.
It's as dark as the insides of wardrobes.

At midday, a man will write a girl's name with his finger
in the dust on a café window. Eventually that's where
we're all heading, dwelling on the river's pitiless flow
or else on some other matter.

How is it that treading in the footsteps of others,
we go astray in search of the infinite
that will open our eyes towards the flame
that has always eluded us? The air degrades
between the balconies, calling to each other
above the streets, and below a shadow, flattened
against the wall, detaches itself, weary of standing.

Elsewhere, someone is madly turning the dial
of a radio, as if hoping it might flower.
First, we must find something to sustain us,
a lasting pact with whatever defeats us least.

Des journées que rien ne traverse

Tu empruntes les grandes routes
pour te séparer de toi-même et voilà qu'un sentier obscur
une boucle imprévisible te ramène à ton vrai visage,
le tien depuis toujours que tu contemples incrédule
et qui t'échappe comme on ne sait quoi d'immatériel sous
   les replis du vent.

Tu as de ces journées que rien ne traverse
à part le flottement du vide, ce sont elles pourtant
qui te réclament le plus par leur effluve d'un silence
   annonceur d'une langue retrouvée,
d'un univers parallèle que le sommeil lentement délivre.

Tu espères te jeter à corps perdu
dans une empreinte de lumière dessinée pour toi seul.

À l'intérieur des frondaisons quelque chose crépite
que tu ne cherches pas à connaître, ni cela ni le temps
dont personne encore ne sait comment il fonctionne.
Peut-être un saut perilleux dans les coulisses de la neige.

Days Where Nothing Happens

You take the main roads to escape from yourself
and out of nowhere, a darkened lane, an unexpected
loop brings you back to your true self,
the face you've always wondered at in disbelief
and which abandons you like some unknown
disembodied thing, bent in the driving wind.

There are days where there's nothing
but the hovering emptiness, but those are the days
that ask the most of you by the reek of their silence
          bringing news of a language recovered
from some remote place, that arrives while you sleep.

You hope to throw yourself bodily
into a pattern of light drawn for you only.

Inside the shrubbery something is rustling,
something you'd rather not see – not *that* – nor time,
whose laws and workings no one can explain.
Would you leap into the fearful corridors of snow?

Entendre les morts est un métier à plein temps

Entendre les morts est un métier à plein temps
et il est surprenant que ne plus les voir
    nous fait déduire qu'ils ont disparu.
Nos souvenirs croient les tenir enfermés alors qu'ils sont
dehors, immensément libres, dans cela qui ne cesse d'advenir.

Ils gardent ce doux langage de la confiance
comme on se parle à soi-même au terme d'une journée
    paisible, toute crainte envolée.

Un songe d'eau fluide les prolonge
sur le lieu où nous sommes quand du verbe fleurit,
dans un pacte de foison lorsqu'un mot s'éclaire d'un autre mot,
    porte plus loin, vers l'ensuite
    où des ondes se répondent.
Leur lumière s'est mise debout
et quelquefois, à travers elle, leurs yeux croisent les nôtres.

Listening to the Dead is Full-time Work

Listening to the dead is full-time work.
How odd it is, that unable to see them,
we believe that they have disappeared.
Our memories would keep them locked away
although in fact they are here at the door,
totally absolved, in the everlasting future.

They observe the mild, confidential tone
that we use when we talk to ourselves
at the end of a quiet day,
when fear has left.

A trickle of thought assures
their continuance and we're back in the zone
where words cluster in the promise of harvest,
and each one is lit by its neighbour,
　　　　and on, towards the hereafter
　　　　where shadows converse.
Their radiance stands upright
and inside it, their eyes sometimes meet ours.

Expectative de l'imprévu

Bateaux de mer, bateaux de mare
sur l'eau écrivent chacun son récit par le sillage.

Ephémères également les roses debout dans le vase
qui ne retiennent leur éclat non plus,
fleurs-mystères d'un feu fugace posé au milieu de la table
à combattre de tout le courage de leurs pétales
            la grandissante obscurité
dans les après-midi de courte lumière

et nos heures en avant se bousculent
vers l'infini des pertes et des fuites.
Nos lendemains se pressent
alors nous hissons des voiles imaginaires
            pour se donner contenance,
rangeons des affaires, histoire de s'occuper.
Ni gai ni triste nous prenons la poussière des meubles
deux fois de suite, prêt à tromper l'ennui,
aux aguets de l'imprévu qui viendra
ou se fera désirer mais sera de coutume attendu.

In Expectation of the Unforeseen

Boats at sea, boats on the mere
write stories on water in their wakes,

ephemeral as roses, upright in the vase,
unable to hold on to their radiance,
ghostly blooms of dying fire set in the middle of the table,
marshal brave petals against
      the gathering dark
in the short-lit afternoon

and the hours ahead jostle for position
towards an eternity of losses and desertions.

Our tomorrows press onward
and we hoist imaginary sails
to keep ourselves on course,
tidy things away, stay active.

Neither happy nor sad we dust the furniture
twice, staving off boredom,
readying ourselves for the unforeseen that is to come
or make us wait, but which from habit,
we have come to expect.

Glissement de terrain

Je m'installe dans une heure libre – hors de la durée.
J'ai l'esprit sans fioritures, le coeur évasé
et l'âme virginale de n'avoir à ce jour frayé avec zéro credo.
Je suis une âme à prendre comme on dit une fille à marier.
Ame que souvent j'arrose d'une bière blonde qui la redore.

Je savoure la tranquille splendeur du jour ambiant.
En plus, il fait beau, d'ailleurs tout le monde l'affirme
et le répète à foison depuis le matin.
Les tilleuls de l'allée ont leur expression pensive.

Inestimable est la sérénité reçue sans que l'on s'y attendait,
superbe intruse à la façon d'une dentelle de lumière tendre
qui vous câline la joue par inadvertance.
Intérieurement on pépie avec les oiseaux.

On en vient au fait avec soi-même,
la vie nous apparaît sous la forme d'une oeuvre à simplifier
dans le saint oubli de toutes choses apprises.
On se ramène au principal sans autre histoire que la sienne.

    Si la fin dernière me réclame
j'aimerais qu'elle s'apparente à un glissement de terrain
en douceur donnant sur un décor jamais vu auparavant.

Landslide

I settle down in a vacant hour – no need to mark the time.
No need for any embellishment, my heart is light
and I'm pure as a virgin, no doctrine on my mind –
a soul *for the taking,* as I've heard it said of girls ripe
for marriage, a soul that I often refresh with a lager.

How I relish the peaceful splendour of the day.
What's more, it's a *lovely* day, everyone says so
and have gone on saying so since daybreak.
The lime trees have that pensive look I know well.

There's nothing like serenity when you least expect it,
dazzling intruder, patterned in lacy sunlight,
accidentally brushing against your cheek.
Inwardly, one's twittering along with the birds.

And here, you're brought face to face with yourself.
Life appears as a piece of work in need of simplifying
in the blessed abandon of all that you've learned –
at one with the core of the matter and no other story but yours.

     If my time is up, so be it;
I'd like it to resemble a slow motion landslide,
opening softly on a wholly other scene.

L'essentiel incognito

L'essentiel nous échappe,
désespérément ailleurs d'où nous sommes.
Parfois il nous visite
quand nous oublions de fermer une fenêtre
et nous manquons la rencontre car notre souci
est de mettre les affaires tangibles
    à leurs places convenues.
Un cortège de détails nous accapare:
nouer des fragments de ficelle
    autour d'un carton à chaussures
pour en fixer le couvercle, ranger des vêtements
au fond de l'armoire dans le sens prévu, à plat,
manier des ustensiles jusqu'à leur épuisement.

La voix grêle de l'habitude oscille
entre la résignation et la parole
    convoquée au secret du coeur.
Vers quelle direction nous sentirons-nous renaître?
Ce sera une main de sel qui perce le gel,
l'eau réinvestie dans sa vocation de partage.

Essential Incognito

The essential escapes us,
hopelessly elsewhere from where we are.
Sometimes it drops in
when we forget to close a window
and we miss the encounter because our care
is for putting things away
      in their accustomed places.
A procession of detail consumes us:
using lengths of string to tie down
the covers of shoeboxes, laying clothes
flat in the back of a wardrobe,
handling implements until they wear out.

Habit's frail voice oscillates
between renunciation and speech
      convened by the secrets of the heart.
For what purpose will we find ourselves reborn?
It will be a handful of salt piercing the ice,
water replenished in the act of giving.

Jamael

Un poète vécut dans la contrée puis s'en alla.
Appelons-le Jamael. Chez lui pas de porte où frapper,
seulement des sandales qui l'attendent sur le seuil,
prêtes au départ de sa masure en vielles grosses pierres
paysannes posées à plat comme des *o* étendues.

Corps de plume nourri de feu, le rêve prodigue,
il s'engage dans la célébration des confluences,
épouse la tournure de causes limpides
            et sait décrypter l'aster.
Lorsqu'il recontre une gitane ce sont deux hirondelles
heureuses de se revoir après de longues migrations.

Réjoui d'un large éventail d'espaces à ouvrir,
l'allégresse qu'il croyait perdue l'investit à nouveau et
lumineux, indomptable, un écho d'orge vibrante
            s'empresse de le rejoindre.

Jamael a un bras pour connaître l'hiver,
une voix plus dense que la brume.
Ses nuits sont émaillées d'airelles.

Autrefois il était
le battement noir des rafales sur les cimes.

Jamael

A poet once lived in our district. Then left.
We will call him Jamael. There was no door
on which to knock, only a pair of sandals
propped ready for departure on the step of the cottage
built of ancient boulders laid flat
like elongated *Os*.

A feathered body fed by flames, prolific dreamer,
he devotes himself to the harmony of merging streams,
woos the eloquence of plain speech
       and can break the aster's code.
He finds a Romany girl and they are like two swallows
happy together after their long migrations.

A great fan of possibilities opens itself to him,
the bliss he thought was lost returns
and the echo of a rustling sheaf of barley,
luminous, untameable
       hurries to his side.

Jamael has an arm to steer a path through winter,
a voice as sonorous as mist.
His nights are jewelled with wild berries.

In another life he was the battering wind
in the treetops.

La vie tendre

Lorsque je demeure longuement à l'attendre
assis dans un fauteuil, le calme qui m'investit est un genre
      de sacrement.
Cela qui me fût inaccessible à l'extérieur,
je m'affaire à le chercher au dedans de moi.
Plein d'approximations, j'emprunte une mémoire
en forme d'escalier. Des vapeurs se dissipent et

un talus d'herbes molles descend jusqu'en Italie,
je m'abandonne à lui, me laisse porter
avec le sourire d'un enfant ravi
devant sa première bouchée de pain d'épices.
      Je vogue dans la vie tendre
qui ne retient aucun passé, vie de mie blanche où l'on
      s'accorde le temps d'être à soi.

Des sons feutrés m'approchent,
on dirait une balle de tennis rebondissante
ou des nuages quand ils se tamponnent
et c'est mon coeur qui bat sa cadence retrouvée.

The Soft Life

I wait in an armchair for it to arrive
and the calm that engulfs me is a kind of ceremony.
My life is spent searching inside myself
for what I couldn't find in the outside world.
Awash with half-truths, I picture myself in a stairwell
of memories. I choose one, the mist parts

and a soft grassy slope meanders down to Italy,
I surrender to it, let it carry me,
smiling like a small boy,
enjoying his first taste of gingerbread.
        I drift in the soft life —
that remembers nothing of the past,
and yields like the inside of a loaf —
where I take time to be myself.

Muffled sounds approach me,
I'm reminded of the thud of a tennis ball,
or clouds bumping together:
It's my heart beating to its old rhythm.

Me reviennent aujourd'hui

un ruisseau parsemé de minuscules châteaux indestructibles
      au fond de l'onde
un jet de soleil aveuglant la Vierge sur l'icône grecque
      dans l'escalier tournant d'une maison disparue
la visite ponctuelle d'un merle chanteur superbement frère
une pluie sur l'épiderme douce au toucher
l'accueil d'une galette sur la table un matin au son des cloches
des parures écarlates un quinze août qui défilent
la chair sarclée d'un champ sous la peau moelleuse de nimbus

au pied de la colline ce frêne qui persiste à pousser
      lui déjà grand lorsque j'étais petit
une aurore cousue main faite pour durer un siècle
un barde aux strophes admirablement débraillées
le coquelicot solitaire comme un garde rouge dans ma ouche
mes rêves emplis de pas qui s'éloignent
un sphère de brume figée au-dessus de l'étang
une chambre d'hôtel au tapis écru foulé par les insomniaques
le visage de celui que j'étais et à ce jour demeure.

It Comes Back to Me Today

a scattering of miniature fortresses
      in the bed of the stream,
a sunbeam dazzling the Virgin on her icon
      set in the spiral staircase of a vanished house,
the punctual arrival of a singing blackbird
– magnificent brother –
rain falling on skin soft to the touch,
the lure of brioche on the table one morning
to the sound of church bells, scarlet vestments
on the feast of the Assumption paraded
round the field, marked by the foot of the plough
in the dull glow of a halo,

at the foot of the hill, this ash tree,
      so tall when I was a boy, is still growing,
a sunrise, hand-stitched, centuries-old,
a minstrel famed for his shambling verses,
a solitary poppy like a sentinel on my plot,
my dreams filled with receding footsteps,
a ball of mist sitting over the lake,
a hotel room's buff-coloured carpet,
scuffed by the feet of insomniacs, the face
of he that I once was and am still to this day.

Prune sauvage

Je sacralise la prune couchée sur mon chemin
pour la simple raison qu'elle se trouve là où je l'aperçois.
Je la relève de la poussière et c'est elle qui me porte
secours, m'assiste par un effet de magnétisme imprévu.

Je vais dans le sens d'une plume au vent.
Pareil à tout le monde je navigue dans l'invérifiable,
pareil à moi-même je fais semblant de grandir
et comme vous tous je traverse la vie sans la comprendre.

Je suis passionément cela qu'en mon intérieur je prononce,
     bien que l'essentiel reste à dire
      et les vrais mots soient intraduisibles.
Je verrai quel instinct m'arrêtera au bord de quel dévaloir.

Accoudé à ma fenêtre
j'aime savoir la nuée blanche porteuse de mystère
autant que la noire, m'emplir d'une ampleur incertaine –
serait-ce un rayon hésitant sur le carrelage –
et clore mes persiennes avec une infinie lenteur
pour ne pas froisser l'air autour d'elles.

Wild Plum

I celebrate the plum lying on my path
simply because it's there for me to see.
I raise it from the dust and I am rescued
by the force of such unforeseen attraction.

I go as a feather is blown in the wind.
Like everyone, I surf the seas of conjecture.
True to form I tell myself I'm growing,
and like you I live without understanding.

I am passionate about what I have to say
    although the essential remains unsaid
    and the actual words are untranslatable.
What impulse would stop me at the edge of the pit?

Leaning at my window
I love to watch the white mist, envoy of mystery,
as well as the black, and fill myself with hazy majesty —
could it be a sunbeam flickering on the tiles?
and I close the blinds with such infinite slowness
that the air around them suffers no tremor.

Néanmoins

Il faut se rendre aux mots
dans un contentement chantonné,
les lèvres mi-closes, sans brusquerie,
être à soi-même comme le chat assis sous le pommier.
Suivre le glissement de la lune et ne se préoccuper de
rien d'autre.

Mais la sérénité est un continent inabordable,
un train qui n'arrive pas, un messie en panne,
et nous restons debout à des carrefours
encombrés de questions imprécises et
de réponses improbables, en peine de choisir.
Nous avons néanmoins une candeur immense à investir
du même élan, du même allant qu'à l'époque où nous
étions petits.

Nous sommes des conglomérats de molécules sacralisés par
l'espoir d'une éclaircie,
des rêveurs de promesses démurées.
Nous saluons d'une main le soleil bifurquant derrière l'épaule
de la montagne et de l'autre accueillons la nuit comme une soeur.
Chaque parole nous sert de sésame. Aucun geste n'est dérisoire.
Le moindre fragment d'une existence vaut d'être repris
et consigné sous la forme d'une perle rare.

Nous distinguons désormais les moments trempés d'absolu
qui nous sont offerts.
Pour commencer, ne fermons plus les cercles que nous traçons
sur le papier, la plage, l'espace aérien et n'importe où.

In Spite of Everything

We must surrender to words with a light heart,
lips half-closed, without abruptness,
at ease with ourselves like a cat under the apple tree,
watching the moon sliding past,
with no other thought on our minds.

But serenity is a distant continent,
a train that won't come, a prophet stuck in traffic,
and we stand at various crossroads weighed down
with imprecise questions
and unlikely answers, struggling to decide.
In spite of everything we are possessed by a desire
for the truth, that is felt with the kind of zeal and fervour
      that we felt as children.

We are conglomerates of molecules endowed
      with the wish for enlightenment,
dreamers of limitless promises.
With one hand we salute the sun as it veers away behind
the mountainside and with the other we greet the night like a sister.
Any word can be used as a password. No gesture is meaningless.
The smallest fragment of a life is worth revision
and must be valued as a rare jewel.

From now on each one of us will be able to say: *this is the absolute*
      moment, among the moments I was given.
How to start? We'll give up closing the circles that we draw
on paper, on sand, in the open air and everywhere else.

Observations durant la journée

Mai arrive en avance. Je n'éprouve plus aucun désert en moi
et chaque visage que je croise m'en rappelle aussitôt un autre.

Nous sommes plusieurs à chercher une solution probable,
quêteurs d'alliances crédibles voués à réduire les distances.
        Plusieurs à propager la force de l'oeil ouvert.

Dans le parc un gamin muni d'un bâton dessine un losange,
se couche au milieu et fixe le bleu myosotis du firmament.

J'arrondis les racines carrées, j'accompagne telle ligne incurvée
au plus étrange qu'elle voudra m'entraîner.
Parmi les pensées qui me survolent je retiens la plus alléchante.

Le chantonnement des roses me fait tourner la tête
vers sa provenance. Je dépose mes armes devant leur charme.
Les fleurs accèdent à l'immortalité par l'ombre gravée sur le sol.

Je souris à mon reflet devant les vitrines comme si m'observait
un illustre inconnu drôlement fagoté. Je vais et viens
animé de considérations nobles et triviales qui se mélangent
en cette sarabande bigarée à laquelle je me suis habitué.

Je caresse dans le sens du poil* deux ou trois idées à mûrir
ainsi qu'une pêche velue assise sur le dressoir depuis mon lever.

Today's Observations

May has come early. The desert within me has lifted
and each face I meet instantly reminds me of another.

Some of us are cogitating on a feasible answer,
a sworn promise to lessen the distance between us,
       a pledge to keep our eyes open.

In the park a boy, armed with a stick, marks out a diamond
and lies down on it, staring up at the forget-me-not blue
of the sky.

I round up square roots, follow whatever curve
that tries to drag me to all that is most strange.
From the thoughts that waft over me,
I choose the most delectable.

The hum of roses makes me turn my head
towards its provenance. I am helpless in front of their charm.
The shadow etched in the ground assures their immortality.

I smile at myself in shop windows as if watched
by some illustrious nobody, fancily got up. I come and go,
enlivened by thoughts, a blend of the lofty and humdrum,
in the courtly dance that has become my habit.

I comfort myself with two or three ideas, mellowing
like the downy peach on the dresser this morning.

Le nom gravé

Un arpège de piano en sourdine
dans une chambre au bout du couloir prélude à l'automne.
      La clarté du jour se condense,
        elle a un jaune d'amadou.
Des ombres se promènent toutes seules, c'est-à-dire
sans forme humaine qui les suit ou les précède.
Chaque chose semble investie d'une raison précise.

L'air sera bientôt fourmillant d'attentes,
La lune d'octobre se laissera pousser la barbe
        afin d'avoir les joues au chaud.

Je reprendrai mes visites au cimetière, je répandrai
        mes pensées sur l'humus refroidi.
Pour l'occasion je me suis offert un complet marron:
autant être bien vêtu devant ceux qui ne le sont plus.

Si la brume ne m'obstrue pas la gorge
à mi-voix je chanterai un psaume de David.
J'en choisirai un de rassurant pour tous, moi inclus.
Mieux, j'inventerai mes propres versets
      sur l'infime que la vie nous apporte
      et suffit néanmoins à la remplir.

The Name, Engraved

Muffled piano scales, announcing Autumn,
reach me from a room at the end of the passage.
      Day light foments
      to a tindery yellow.
Shadows walk around on their own —
with no human form in front or behind.
Each object seems infused with its precise purpose.

A swarm of imminences is coming.
The October moon is growing a beard
to warm its cheeks.

I'll go back to my cemetery walks; I'll scatter
      my thoughts on the chilled earth.
I've ordered myself a brown suit for the occasion;
I might as well be properly attired among those that aren't.

If the fog does not choke me
I'll hum one of the Psalms of David,
under my breath, to reassure everyone, myself included.
Better still, I'll write something of my own
      on all the minutiae of life that paradoxically
      suffice to fill it.

En partant je saluerai la compagnie,
les miens mais aussi les inconnus – eux dont j'ai croisé
tant de fois le nom gravé dans la pierre ou le bois
        qu'ils en sont devenus presque des amis.

Un ou deux amours inoffensifs me divertiront,
de ceux-là qui ne raient pas la surface du coeur
plus fragile quand l'hiver se présente.
        J'essaierai d'écrire un livre et d'en lire cent.

Je renaîtrai au monde le printemps venu
        déposé en offrande à mes pieds.
J'aurai l'intérieur du crâne tapissé d'une mousse verdoyante,
me mettrai en route vers un pays précieux, bienvenu
comme un raisin sec dans la chair d'une galette.

On leaving, I'll wave to the company,
my people and those unknown to me – those
whose names, engraved on stone or wood,
I've passed a hundred times
and who have become almost my friends.

I'll amuse myself with a harmless love affair or two,
the kind that leaves the heart unscathed,
now more fragile as winter approaches.
I will write a book and read a hundred.

My rebirth will take place in Spring –
          set down as a gift at my feet.
The inside of my skull will be carpeted with green moss.
I'll set out on the road to a cherished country,
where I'll be welcomed
like a currant in a bun.

à quoi sert l'amour qui ne dure qu'une vie?
what is the point of love that only lasts a lifetime?
From *Grandeur nature*, p. 17

AFTERWORD TO A SELECTION OF POEMS
BY JACQUES TORNAY

I met Jacques Tornay in 2016 at HeadRead, the International Literary Festival of Estonia. Sitting in the audience, listening to poems in tongues that were foreign to me, I was transported by the familiar sounds of the French. Having been brought up on the poems of Ronsard, Du Bellay, Lamartine, Verlaine and de Regnier, I had the sensation of inhabiting that part of myself that breathes, hears and dreams in French. While the poet spoke, the hubbub of chairs and glasses quietened and I was overtaken by an irresistible smile. After the festival, Jacques sent me copies of his collections and, with his co-operation, I began to translate his poems into English. Some have been published in *Poetry London* and *Modern Poetry in Translation*.

Tornay was a French-speaking Swiss writer, journalist and translator whose work includes poetry, novels, essays, short stories, aphorisms and biography. He was the author of numerous books and the recipient of prestigious prizes, notably the Prix Louise Labé 1993, the Prix de la Société des Gens de Lettres de France 2002 and 2010 and the Prix de la Loterie Romande 2003 and 2018. As a freelance cultural commentator, he was a frequent visitor to the UK and received a diploma in translation from the University of Cambridge. He spent some years in Berne as a translator and collaborated with press agencies and journals on matters cultural and philosophical. He presented *Bateau Livre,* a literary radio programme on Radio Rhône. His poems have appeared in many anthologies, in particular with Editions Seghers in 2008/9. He took part in poetry festivals in Switzerland and worldwide and sat on judging panels of literary prizes, among them the Prix Pierrette Micheloud (Lausanne), the Grand Prix International de Poesie de langue francaise, Leopold Sedar-Senghor de la Nouvelle Pléiade (Paris), and the Prix Rainer Maria Rilke (Sierre). He was president of la Société des Ecrivains Valaisans from 2009 to 2017. In 2008, he received the Palmes Academiques (section Suisse) granted by Ministère Français de l'Education Nationale, and in 2011, la Medaille d'Or de la Renaissance Française. Jacques died on 6 February 2019 after a short illness. I feel his loss very keenly. Christina Holm Tornay, his widow, has been a great, almost daily source of comfort to me, and I to her, as we mourn his passing, discuss fine points of his work and recall his qualities and idiosyncrasies. Her friendship sustains me.

During the last three years in which I have been translating his poems into English, I found myself inhabiting the 'talked-about world' of Rilke's *Duino Elegies,* in which:

> . . . we aren't really at home . . .
> So we're left with say, some tree on a hillside –
> One that we see every day; we're left with yesterday's
> stroll and the pampered loyalty of an old habit
> that liked us so much it decided to stay, and never left.

And it was no surprise to learn of his love of Rilke, the poet he most reminds me of. When I found the line in 'Wild Plum':

> And like you, I live without understanding,

I was struck by how often that thought appears in his work, in different forms. And, as with Rilke, a sense of the sacred is always present, at times placid and luminous, at others forlorn and recalcitrant. I do not mean that this is his subject matter, but rather that, in his entire oeuvre, there is the *sous-entendu* of some (divine) force animating all things and places and all beings and their states, meanings, actions and interactions, and component parts, even at their darkest. When, in 'In Spite of Everything' he writes,

> The smallest fragment of a life is worthy of revision
> and must be treasured like a rare jewel

you know that he means it, even if you find yourself wondering: *Really? The smallest fragment?*

Set in the mountainous landscapes of his native country, these are poems of ontological introspection and the enigma of the self. They explore opposing states of being human: serenity, anxiety; enlightenment, delusion; conviction, uncertainty; mundanity, exaltation – *and* their ephemeral nature. This is a poet who is concerned with those mysteries that are real.

Their iconography includes domestic animals, streams, small huts, the occasional cupboard, the wind, particular trees, a teapot handle, repetitive household tasks, days, habits, waiting, vacancy, going away from and returning home, settling down for the afternoon, talking to oneself, the sound of a piano, the weather, the sky, the night, the seasons, a neighbour, the topography of his native land and cake. As they become familiar, the reader registers these landmarks, as having the kind of forensic quality that is found in Proust.

Tornay's poems are charged with an unremitting, almost Sisyphus-like sense of ordinariness and everydayness. Whether recalling a wild plum lying on his path, the smell of pickled cabbage or the task of putting away last season's clothes, the reader is aware not only of a strange and unique quality of stoicism but also a slow release of philosophical largesse. In the poem 'Jamael', the reader is offered an 'arm to steer a path though Winter.'

They reveal an often disconcerting capacity for conveying simultaneously, in a very few words, the particular *and* the universal – without display, grandiosity or ambiguity – or even eliciting an *Aha!* from the reader. In 'De Si Longues Distances', the seemingly blunt line

On se crée sa legende,

carries the sense that each one fits their own words to whatever particular hymn is being sung – *and* that each of us creates their own version of everything, the two dimensions sitting companionably on the same line.

The principal human presence in almost all of Tornay's poems is that of a 'Je', the 'I', without pretension or vanity – as cumulatively, 'I' deploys its states of being, hopes, preoccupations, pleasures and fears to the reader, an exploration reminiscent of the reflections of the Jewish theologian Martin Buber on the creation of the self:

The basic word I-Thou can be spoken only with one's whole being. The concentration and fusion into a whole being can never be accomplished by me, can never be accomplished without me. I require a Thou to become; becoming I, I say Thou.
All actual life is encounter.

from *Being and Time*

Encounter is what Jacques Tornay's poems deliver. At the point of engagement, the reader experiences a journey into an internal landscape, with a sense of the ineluctable, reminiscent of Dante:

But serenity is a distant continent,
a train that won't come, a prophet stuck in traffic
and we stand at various crossroads,
burdened with imprecise questions and unlikely answers,
struggling to decide.

Many of these poems are spoken in the first person plural, *we*; one of his collections bears the title, *La Premiere Personne du Pluriel*. I believe that the meaning of this 'nous' is to say — but without any particular position or insistence — that we are human beings, no more, no less; that we are many, and that we live on earth with the plants and the animals — and that everything that is, both good and ill, flows from this condition.

At the beginning of my acquaintance with Tornay's poems, I had the idea that the ever-present quest for serenity had to do with the attempt to recover from a particular, but unnamed, personal trauma; and there are, in places, some terrifyingly haunted passages. I now understand that what he means is actually the trauma of being human. When the quest for serenity finds its rare reward, the sense is one of devastating release.

NOTES

1 Hiddensee, pronounced *Hiddenzay*, is a sea-horse-shaped island
   on the Baltic coast of Germany, famed for the instability of its shores,
   the many writers and artists who found sanctuary there, its varied
   architecture, the amber to be found on its beaches, sunny climate
   and relaxed way of life. It takes its name from the legendary King
   Hedin, whose conquest of the lands of King Högni, abduction of his
   daughter and the ensuing Battle of the Hjadnings are recounted in
   the ancient Skaldic poem 'Ragnarsdrdpa' and later in the fifteenth-
   century manuscript Flateyjarbók. The largest discovery of Viking
   gold artefacts ever found in Germany, believed to have belonged to
   the Danish King Harald Bluetooth, took place on Hiddensee during
   reconstruction after flooding in 1872. The image on the frontispiece
   is a painting I made in 2016 of the house on Hiddensee, modelled on
   a photograph taken by my grandmother in 1933.

2 Cobra Mist was the codename for an Anglo-American experimental
   over-the-horizon radar station at Orford Ness, Suffolk (grid reference
   TM450511).

3 The etymology of the mondegreen:
      In a 1954 essay in *Harper's* magazine, the American writer Sylvia
   Wright described how, as a young girl, she misheard the line from
   the ballad 'The Bonnie Earl of Moray', 'and laid him on the green' as
   'and Lady Mondegreen'. Wright explains the need for a new term,
   as follows: *The point about what I shall hereafter call mondegreens,
   is that they are better than the original.*

This particular mondegreen originates from a story told to me by Jon Sayers in which I heard him recall someone intending to mention the song 'Somewhere Over the Rainbow', saying 'Rimbaud's Ovaries' instead. However Jon has no recollection of it.

4 The carving of the woman, the baptismal font and other figures are to be found in the eleventh-century church of St Mary of the Assumption in Ufford, Suffolk.

5 'In the Street of Knives', *New Collected Poems*, ed. Matthew Francis (London: Faber, 2004), p. 309. A recording of W. S. Graham reading this poem can be found at: https://warwick.ac.uk/fac/arts/scapvc/about/archive/writers/wsgraham/231079, where I first found it. Recalling a memory of my own visit to the Street of Knives in Heraklion, I used Graham's poem as the model for mine.

6 There are two sources for this poem. The first is the title of a doctoral research paper on the technology of gesture authentication in financial transactions and its influence on human interaction. The second is a glossary of seafaring terms.

7 Maurice Scève was a French poet active in Lyon during the Renaissance period. He was at the centre of the Lyonnese literary côterie that elaborated the theory of spiritual love, derived partly from Plato and partly from Petrarch. Having sunk into oblivion, interest in his oeuvre revived during the nineteenth century.

8 The Valais is a canton in southern Switzerland.

9 The optative is a mood for verbs in the ancient Greek language, used to express wishes, curses and prayers.

10 *Le Malade Imaginaire* is a comedy by Molière.

11 The Fendant is a popular white wine of the Valais region.

12 *Les Barricades Mystérieuses* is a collection of poems by Olivier Larronde, active in the 1940s and 50s and is also the title of a piece of music for harpsichord, composed in 1717 by François Couperin.

13 Roughly translates as: *It was so-o-o-o fucked!*

14 Dudes.

15 *Chapeau Melon et Bottes de Cuir*, literally Bowler Hat and Leather Boots, was the title given to the French-language broadcast of *The Avengers*.

16 In Victorian times, leporellos were concertina-style postcards, printed with images of popular tourist destinations. This binding technique takes its name from Mozart's opera *Don Giovanni*, in which his servant, Leporello, confronts his master with a written tally of his many seductions. The text is an extract from *English Hours* by Henry James.

17 A *calembour* is a play on words in which a word or phrase is unconsciously misheard and reproduced to convey a quite different meaning. The term comes from the name Count Kahlenberg, a nineteenth-century German diplomat to Paris, whose pronunciation made it so difficult for him to be understood that his interlocutors were only able to make the loosest interpretations of his proposals. 'Tohu wa-bohu' is a biblical Hebrew phrase found in the Genesis creation narrative that describes the condition of the earth immediately before the creation of light. In French, it is used to mean hurly-burly, such as in a crowded airport terminal.

   The phrase 'Le toyboy de tohu-bohu' came up in a conversation between myself, Christina Holm Tornay and Padraig Rooney, in which I misheard the Hebrew expression 'Tohu-Bohu' as 'Toyboy'. It seemed a suitable moniker for Boris Johnson.

18 Antonella da Messina's small but magnificent painting of St Jerome can be viewed here: http://www.nationalgallery.org.uk/paintings/ antonello-da-messina-saint-jerome-in-his-study

* One of the delights of translating poetry is finding hitherto undiscovered words and expressions that possess a unique piquancy. *'Foucade'*, derived from the Latin *'fugere'*, to flee, and which translates approximately as caprice or whim, is one. *'Caresser dans le sens du poil'*, which translates literally as 'to stroke with the grain' and means 'to flatter', is another.

ACKNOWLEDGEMENTS AND THANKS

The author wishes to thank the editors of *Poetry London*, *Modern Poetry in Translation*, *Poetry Review*, *Long Poem Magazine*, the Poetry Business, *Ambit* and *The Caught Habits of Language* (Donut Press) in which earlier versions of some of these poems have appeared.

Particular gratitude is due to the late Jacques Tornay for his permission to publish my translations of his poems as follows:

From *Feuilles de présence* – Editions L'Arrière Pays – 2006
'L'essentiel incognito'
'Jamael'
'Néanmoins'

From *Gains de causes* – Editions L'Arrière Pays – 2009
'Ce qui nous dépossède le moins'
'Entendre les morts est un métier à plein temps'
'Des journées que rien ne traverse'
'La vie tendre'
'Prune sauvage'

From *A parts entières* – Editions de l'Aire – 2018
'Expectative de l'imprévu'

'Me reviennent aujourd'hui'
'Observations durant la journée'
'Glissement de terrain'

'Le nom gravé' – 2018 – uncollected

Thanks are also due to the following for their encouragement and advice: Don Paterson, Rachael Boast, Rachael Clyne, Giovanni Aloi, Catherine Lampert, Claire Feasey, Elaine Beckett, Christina Holm Tornay, Stéphane Bochatay, Chris Beckett, Dorothy Elford, Tamar Yoseloff, the Cattistock Poetry Group, the Helyars and Art2Card for digital imaging.